THE CHURCH OF GOMORRAH

The Church of Gomorrah

WHEN SEXUAL ABUSERS REMAIN IN THE CHURCH

Deanna Christian Wendy Hoke

Melanie Jula Sakoda

eWriterUSA

Copyright © 2022 Deanna Christian & Wendy Hoke

Published by eWriterUSA

Cover Design by Wendy Hoke

No part of this book may be reproduced except in brief quotations and in reviews without written permission from the publisher.

10 9 8 7 6 5 4 3 2 1

The Book of Gomorrah
2022, Deanna Christian & Wendy Hoke

EWriterUSA.com

Dedication

Deanna Christian dedicates this book to her beloved niece, Kimberly, who has always been a blessing, and to all children with the hope that they will be safe from sexual predators and not further abused by their church's inappropriate response.

Wendy Hoke dedicates this book to her charming, cheerful son, McKinley. May he always be safe from predators. May he always have faith in truth.

"Satan doesn't fight against the Church.
Satan joins the Church."

-Wendy Hoke

The Bishop's Cross

Foreward

The true prevalence of childhood sexual abuse is difficult to determine because it is often not reported. Statistical numbers of what is known, however, are staggering: One in five girls and one in 20 boys are victims of sexual abuse in the United States. Most abuse happens in the hands of family members, religious authorities, and/or people known to the victims.

The truth about the abuse is often found in the memories of people undergoing counseling for post-traumatic stress disorders years after the events took place. In this context, most perpetrators go unpunished: No moral, social, or legal justice is served. Victims are often left to deal with life-long psychological and relational damage without experiencing any sense of retributive justice. Victims are permanently wounded and often labeled as "crazy" by deniers, by religious authorities, and by family members, and others. Many times, these childhood victims of sexual abuse find no support or credence in their families and faith communities, which contributes to the establishment of a long-term "conspiracy of silence."

This process of re-traumatization of the victim is exacerbated when the abuser is a member of a religious congregation or—even worse--of the clergy. Most victims remain silent for years and their entire relationship with others, with God, and with their churches, is marred. Child victims are intimidated by the potential repercussions of speaking up against those perceived by others as "representatives of God on earth." These children are often accused of lying, exaggerating, and distorting the truth--even by close members of their families such as parents and siblings. All of these mistaken social attitudes constitute victim-bashing and are done to maintain the status quo of the family and of the religious congregation.

While these activities continue and go unpunished leaving a trail of hapless victims behind, the perpetrators habitually find refuge in the positions taken by religious authorities. Not infrequently, perpetrators have been helped by the leaders of their churches who are supposed to prevent abuse. Clerical authorities in all churches often justify the abusers' behaviors, keeping them secret from others. This has been done in the name of protecting "the sacredness of confession" and the promotion of the ideology of "the regeneration of the sinner." These leaders have misapplied New Testament notions of "mercy and forgiveness" and have allowed unscrupulous people to stay on in their churches after they have been identified as sexual perpetrators. This "forgiving" attitude has become an open door for the sexual abuse of children in all Christian denominations, of which the best-known cases are those of priests in the Catholic church. But the actual size of the problem in American society is much larger, and it involves families and communities and their own reactions to the abuse of the child. This code of silence has led to thousands of cases never being reported to the lay authorities, which has worked for the long-term protection of the perpetrators' impunity.

In *The Church of Gomorrah*, the authors Deanna Christian and Wendy Hoke, tell the stories of abuse by family members and religious authorities. They break "the conspiracy of silence" taking on whatever repercussions may come their way. In this seminal book geared towards Christian leadership—and any other reader interested in this subject-- they describe the growing problem of sexual child abuse in religious communities across the United States. They examine the attitudes churches and family members often take regarding children who dare report abuse. The authors show how erroneous family attitudes exacerbate the problem rather than help children be protected in the situation and allowed to heal. The book goes on to examine in depth this matter from a Scriptural perspective.

The authors make the point of the importance of retributive justice. This justice must be applied without exception to these cases. These injunctions are based on Old Testament and New Testament commands. These commands demand that those who incur these sins on children must be brought out into the light, exposed to others and the law, and expelled from their congregations. In the eyes of the authors, this is the right Christian stance—regardless of church denomination--when confronted with this unspeakable evil.

This book then stresses the need to change current prevailing attitudes in churches regarding these actions. The authors call for a radical Biblical-based change in religious authorities. This means going from an attitude of silencing victims, and attempting to debunk their reports, to one in which accused people be investigated--and when perpetrators are found--be exposed and expelled. The message of *The Church of Gomorrah* is clear: A mandate must be sent to all by all church authorities and from the pulpits: There is no room for any kind of sexual abuse in churches, let alone of children. And church policy in this matter must change to support the victims of childhood sexual abuse in their healing process while exerting a zero-tolerance policy for the permanence of perpetrators in their communities of faith.

—Rodolfo A. Trivisonno, MD

Introduction

The Bible gives us unequivocal instructions regarding certain sexual sins. Yet, churches everywhere have failed to follow those instructions for millennia. This book looks at the global problem of child sexual abuse committed by priests, pastors, and others in authority within the Christian church.

We begin with the Roman Catholic Church (RCC) because it has garnered far more headlines with scandals that shock the senses. We also show that child sexual abuse occurs in other Christian denominations. The response in nearly all churches is the same: allow the abuser to be "forgiven" and remain in the church. However, is this what the Bible commands?

How bad is the contemporary pedophile priest problem in the RCC? The scandals span across many countries: Australia, Ireland, the U.S., and more. The Catholic Church has faced a massive flood of child sexual abuse accusations over the last several decades. Wikipedia has an entire page dedicated to Catholic Church sexual abuse cases by country, which lists 23 countries with documented cases of child sexual abuse by priests.

As the current scandals continue, the alleged cover-ups continue as well. Victim groups demand more action from the Vatican to remove pedophile priests and right the wrongs. In an effort to address the problem, Pope Francis recently held an unprecedented summit on pedophilia in the Church.

A few accusations came to light in the 1950s. Child molestation by Catholic priests received more media reporting in the 1980s in the U.S. and Canada.

In the 1990s, accusations began growing in Argentina and Australia. In 1995, the Archbishop of Austria, Hans Hermann Groer, resigned amid child sexual abuse allegations that rocked the Catholic Church there. Concurrently, allegations of widespread abuse in Ireland made the news. By the early 2000s, child sexual abuse by pedophile priests was revealed as a major global crisis.

In the United States in 2002, The Boston Globe exposed widespread child sexual abuse by priests in Boston, Massachusetts, and uncovered how Church leaders transferred the offending priests around to avoid accountability and cover up the problem. As the Globe printed more headlines, more victims came forward in the U.S. and around the world.

The Church's response included Pope Francis calling for "decisive action" when he was elected in 2013. In 2018, he wrote to all members of the church condemning clergy sexual abuse of children and calling for an end to cover-ups. He abolished the secrecy policy allowing the Church to share information with local law enforcement. Yet, scripture tells us to put the abuser out of the church. It does not tell us to hide the truth and transfer offending priests to other parishes.

We argue in this book that the never-ending promises and rare actions taken by the Roman Catholic Church and other Christian denominations are not based on scripture. We will look at the problems of pedophile priests/pastors and incest. We believe that sexual sins within the Church are forms of incest as we are all children of God, brothers and sisters in Christ, and one family of believers. The Bible, both the old and new testaments, are clear on how to address sexual sin.

In addition, we have included several testimonies from adults who were sexually abused as children. We believe this discussion needs to include the voices of victims to gain a greater understanding of the damage and pain that child sexual abuse causes. Some of the testimonies are quite painful. It is necessary to understand the lasting consequences of child sexual abuse.

1

[Delay, Deny, Defend]

Since its beginning, the Roman Catholic Church has made attempts to correctly address sexual sins in the Church. Below is a brief review of some major highlights of those attempts. However, the Church made a critical change in 1866 to its policies that fostered secrecy and allowed priests to retain their positions. This change is in direct opposition to scripture. And, its prior efforts were ineffective and half-hearted. Keep in mind that many contemporary churches in various denominations have histories similar to the one below.

It's tempting to frame this problem as a contemporary evil with a focus on the role, liability, responsibility, and response of the Church towards child sexual abuse committed by clergy members. However, the issue of sexual sin in the church goes back millennia. Successive papal authorities, church laws, and other church procedures have condemned child sexual abuse. Putting those policies into action has taken a certain amount of administrative management that ultimately failed.

Let's take a look at history to understand the central administrative management and how it was developed by the Church after the Second Council of Lateran in 1139. This gave the Papacy administrative control over the greater Church resulting in the formation of organizational structures that could address child sexual abuse between the 14th and 20th centuries.

First, we must acknowledge that the culture surrounding the early Church celebrated man-boy sexual relations (pederasty), and sex between a master and his pupil was the epitome of Greek philosophical learning.

In Rome, a citizen could exploit his own slaves for sex regardless of age or gender. A freeborn Roman could torture, rape, or abuse their slaves without charge or prosecution. Boys born or sold into slavery, captured in war, or even freed slaves were frequently exploited and used for the sexual gratification of their masters. It was considered socially acceptable to sexually abuse young male slaves in debased acts of pederasty by the elites of Roman men.

Early Christians took the opposite view based on Jewish law. The apostle Paul condemned all sexual sins by Christians including sexual immorality, homosexuality, and adultery, although this book is specific to child sexual abuse and incest. In 1 Corinthians, Paul states that men who participated in these activities would not inherit the kingdom of God. Paul went further than that, commanding the Church to expel the abuser and turn him over to Satan until the Day of the Lord.

How has the Roman Catholic Church addressed child sexual abuse? Let's review.

A Brief Review of the RCC's Attempts to Address Sexual Sin

While reviewing dry historical dates can make our eyes glaze over, it's important to consider this brief overview in relation to the depths of the problem and the shocking change in policy in 1866.

The Roman Catholic Church (RCC) is over 2,000 years old, and it has made some attempts to correctly address sexual sins in the Church. However, the RCC made a critical change to its policies in 1866 that fostered secrecy and allowed priests to retain their positions. This change is in direct opposition to scripture.

Evidence exists that the RCC has a history of CSA that goes back centuries. At the same time, successive papal authorities, church laws, and other Church procedures have condemned CSA. Yet, putting policies into action takes a certain amount of administrative management. One must look at history to understand that the central administrative management was developed by the Church after the Second Council of Lateran in 1139. This gave the Papacy administrative control over the greater Church resulting in the formation of organizational structures that could address CSA (and other issues) between the 14th and 20th centuries.

How has the Church addressed CSA?

For the first 11 centuries, the Church issued many instructions for Christians to stay away from pederasty (and other sexual sins). The consequences were to withhold communion even at death. In his letter to Pope Leo IX in 1049, St. Peter Damian (1007-1072) stated:

> "Any cleric or monk who seduces young men or boys, or who is apprehended in kissing a woman shall be publicly flogged ... he shall be disgraced by spitting in his face, bound in iron chains, wasted by six months of close confinement, and for three days each week put on barley bread given him toward evening. Following this period, he shall...[live] in

a small segregated courtyard in custody of a spiritual elder, kept busy with manual labor, subjected to vigils and prayers, forced to walk at all times in the company of two spiritual brothers, never again allowed to associate with young men."

This mirrors instructions attributed to St. Basil (330-379 C.E.)

"A cleric or monk who seduces youths or young boys...is to be publicly flogged...For six months he will languish in prison-like confinement... and he shall never again associate with youths in private conversation nor in counseling them."

Note that neither of the instructions suggested putting the priest out of the church essentially firing him, thus defrocking and excommunicating him.

Suggested punishments also included imprisonment of 7 years for deacons, 10 years for priests, and 12 years for bishops. Some documents from the Council of Nicaea (325 C.E.) prevented pedophile priests from practicing in the ministry. Other documents suggested that pedophile priests were transferred around as early as the second and third centuries. That practice began early, not just in the 20th century.

There were also warnings of divine punishment. St. Peter Damian in *The Book of Gomorrah* argued for much stronger punishments for pedophile priests, and he called on Pope Leo IX to expel them.

Regarding sodomy, Damian wrote: "unquestionably this vice, since it passes the enormity of others, is impossible to compare with any other vice. It brings death to the body and destruction to the soul."

In fact, according to Peter Payer, who translated Damian's treatise, "*The Book of Gomorrah* stands out as a carefully planned and eloquently executed discussion of the subject reflecting both a legalistic concern with correct ecclesiastical censure and a passionate pastoral concern for those caught up in the behavior."

Why the Church hasn't followed his urgings, the apostle Paul's exhortations and laws in Leviticus is, unfortunately, an unanswered question.

While Pope Leo IX agreed that clergy guilty of sexual sin should be dismissed from service, this rarely happened in practice. Some were dismissed under Pope Leo IX, but others were urged to repent. Sound familiar?

What happened when the Vatican took a lenient stance on various sexual sins? The practice of child sexual abuse, sodomy, and other Church-recognized sexual sins spread freely. It may be that the habit of looking the other way began during this time period. In modern parlance, we call it "delay, deny, defend." The RCC undoubtedly had the laws and policies in place to address these concerns dating back to the earliest days of the Church. A collection of these policies was compiled in the 12th century called the Decretum Gratiani, which laid out the Church laws regarding child sexual abuse, casual sex, adultery, homosexuality, and clerical concubinage. It also called for the banishment or capital punishment of those who committed sexual abuse of minors depending on what actually happened. It called for dismissal or ex-communion for offending clergy, and it deemed pedophile activity to be a crime based on canon law. That remained in effect until the Code of Canon Law of 1917.

The Lateran Councils

The RCC continued to recognize sexual sins. The Third Lateran Council (1179) called for dismissal or confinement to a monastery for life. The Fourth Lateran Council (1215) also called for dismissal or confinement to a monastery for life, which essentially exiled and imprisoned the man if he was found guilty. The Fifth Lateran Council (1514) reiterated the call to put offending priests on trial to be punished if found guilty. The Council of Trent (1545-1563) required Bishops to punish priests for sexual sins, dismiss them, and hand them over to secular authorities for punishment.

Based on the number of times the Church addressed the issue during various Councils, it can be argued that the Church had a serious, ongoing problem.

Some estimates put the rate of clergy child sexual abuse close to 25% although clergy made up only about 2% of the population. In one case, Pope Julius III (1487-1555) picked up a boy off the street and had sexual relations with him.

In 1561, Pope Pius IV issued "Cum Sicut Nuper, which condemned priests who committed sexual acts during confessions. He called for the guilty priests to be dismissed and handed over to secular authorities.

Just seven years later in 1568, Pope Pius V stated:

> "Whoever commits such an execrable crime (bestiality, pedophilia, sodomy, etc.), by force of the present law be deprived of every clerical privilege, of every post, dignity, and ecclesiastical benefit, and having been degraded by an ecclesiastical judge, let him be immediately delivered to the secular authority to be put to death as mandated by law as the fitting punishment for laymen who have sunk into this abyss"

Even with the continuing acknowledgment of sexual crimes, the practice dogged the RCC for centuries. The Spanish Inquisition considered sexual crimes to be heresy. Pederasty, sodomy, and homosexuality were crimes against nature, and the Inquisition punished the guilty with imprisonment, torture, and execution.

In the 17th century, Pope Gregory XV issued the papal bull, Universi, that expanded the scope of Cum Sicut Nuper to include priests who had sex with penitents, and Pope Benedict XIV condemned priests who used sex as quid pro quo for absolution. Addressing the problem seemed to depend on the country as well. Some research shows that there were approximately 3,775 disciplinary actions against priests for child sexual abuse in Spain and Mexico between 1723 and 1820. That number is astronomical and most likely a tiny fraction of actual instances of clergy CSA.

A Radical Change in 1866

In 1866, the RCC took a radically different stance towards handing over sexual predators to the secular authorities. It changed how the Church hierarchy addressed accusations of sexual misconduct. That year, Pope Pius IX issued instructions calling for absolute secrecy surrounding the Church trials for perpetrators of sexual abuse committed during confession. The instructions called for only ecclesiastical trials, and it deemed the local ordinaries and inquisitors to be the judges who investigated and prosecuted the accused clergy. They were also to mete out the punishment, which was to withdraw powers from those found guilty.

The judges were required to inform penitents to provide information on derelict priests or risk being denied absolution. If those women (or children) were unwilling to come forward, then their confidants were encouraged to tell the hierarchy about any incidents. This appeared to be an effort to determine which allegations were authentic and which were false accusations. If the clergy was found guilty, he would be removed. However, if he admitted his guilt, he would be reconciled with the church through the process of Abjuratio. All of these procedures were kept secret and held strictly within the Church.

The new instructions allowed pedophile priests to remain active if they confessed and repented. The previous instructions for excommunion or dismissal were removed in those cases. And, they ended any role for secular law enforcement in Church affairs with the adoption of absolute secrecy before, during, and after the ecclesiastical investigations and trials. It gave the pedophile priests an "out" through confession without any attention to the needs of the victims. In fact, the instructions provide no guidance on support, healing, or justice for the victims.

Moreover, the approach to the victims during the initial investigation suggested that they wouldn't be believed. Coupled with forgiving the clergy who committed sexual crimes and allowing them to remain in their positions with their crimes kept secret, it's no surprise that the RCC has been riddled with scandals over the last several decades.

More recent Catholic Church CSA cases include:

- In 2019, Australian Cardinal George Pell was found guilty of abusing two choir boys in 1996; he was convicted nine months earlier, but a court initially forbade the press from reporting it. In 2020, Australia's High Court quashed the conviction.
- Theodore McCarrick, a former Roman Catholic Cardinal in the U.S., was defrocked because of allegations that he sexually assaulted a teenager in New York in the early 1970s
- In August 2018, a Pennsylvania grand jury named more than 300 clergy members in a report which found over 1,000 children had been abused
- Australian Archbishop Philip Wilson resigned in July 2018 after being convicted of concealing child sex abuse carried out by another priest.
- Prior to Pope Francis, Pope Benedict XVI was accused of suppressing investigations, which he denied. However, there were serious questions about what Joseph Ratzinger, who became Pope Benedict XVI, knew about a case involving

sexual abuse of 231 boys from the famous Bavarian Catholic boys' choir.
- Prior to Pope Benedict, Pope John Paul II gave Cardinal Bernard Law, who transferred many pedophile priests around in the Boston scandal, a symbolic role in Rome near the Vatican, where he kept his rank.

In 2011, Pope Benedict issued new guidelines telling bishops to report suspected cases to the local police. This changed the previous guidelines set in 1866 to report all cases to Rome. Pope Francis set up a special panel to address pedophile clergy. During a summit in 2019, Pope Francis promised an end to the cover-ups and promised that all clergy sexual abusers would be brought to justice. The victims are still waiting.

This is very clearly the response of the Church regarding contemporary CSA cases: tolerance toward and protection of sexual abusers, and lack of care and justice for the victims.

When we look at the 2000+ year history of the Catholic Church, we see that sexual sins were known and recognized. The Church has had periods of leniency in enforcing its own laws against clerical sexuality, sodomy, and child sex abuse. During other periods, the Church was more consistent with implementing its own measures. However, those times were rare.

Even though the Church can point to many instances in which it condemned child sexual abuse, the changes made in 1866 opened the door for much greater abuse to take place. The adoption of a secrecy policy along with reconciliation for guilty priests enabled the problems to increase. Removing the role of secular law enforcement allowed the hierarchy to transfer problem priests around without detection. The lack of care toward or belief of the victims ensured their silent suffering for decades while other children were abused as well. In a very real way, this official stance of the RCC made children vulnerable to be treated as objects of sexual gratification and at the disposal of the priesthood

2

[Esther's Story]

I grew up in the suburbs of a large metropolis in the 60s and 70s. My family was close knit, and we had large gatherings during the holidays. My maternal grandfather was the "patriarch" and a Christian pastor. He was revered without question.

When I was about 7 years old, he began to take unusual interest in me. When he came to visit, he would bring me flowers. My birthday is in Spring, and he had a lilac tree in his garden. He would shower me with lilacs on my birthday. He gave me chocolates from See's Candy. He didn't do anything like this with others in the family. I was his special target. He was always hugging me or stroking my hair. He would put me on his lap and bounce me up and down inappropriately. He constantly complimented my looks. And when I was at his home without my parents, he would insist that I drink beer along with him. Saying no was not an option.

I can say now that his actions were inappropriate, but at the time I didn't understand. No one stopped him. My mother thought it was cute.

My grandmother passed away when I was nine. That summer, grandpa decided to take the grandkids (five of us) on a lengthy summer vacation in the Midwest. During that trip, various farm families would agree to host some of the kids for a week. There were three girls and two boys. The other two girls were sisters. So, sometimes a family would take the two sisters. Another family would take the two boys. That left me alone with grandpa for a week at a time.

He insisted I drink beer…a lot especially for a small child. Then, he raped me. He threatened me to keep it secret. He said I would be sent back to the adoption agency (I was adopted) if I told anyone how bad I had been.

The memories of being raped were always there, although at the time, they were a bit fuzzy. When my cousins came back from visiting the farms, I was too terrified to say a word.

I froze. My entire life froze. I lived in a constant state of terror that very soon became my "new normal."

I fell into deep depressions as a teen. And, I became very withdrawn. My mother criticized me repeatedly for being this way. She had wanted a cheerleader for a daughter, not a quiet girl content to read alone in my bedroom.

My early adulthood was an exercise in subconsciously running away from everyone and everything. I changed jobs and homes frequently. I dated a man once or twice, then left.

In my late 30s, I cracked. I came crashing out of that frozen state after hearing a specific sound that reminded me of my head banging against the wall as grandpa raped me. The depths of that crash cannot be overstated. I was diagnosed with PTSD. It took me years to climb back from that fall.

It wasn't until my 40s that I could even begin to address the sexual assault. I couldn't even say the words until my early 50s. When I was 57, I finally went public even though I knew that doing so meant I would be forever ostracized from my family. Grandpa was considered to be just about perfect...never to be questioned or criticized.

Speaking out meant shaming the family according to my adoptive mother.

When I announced that I was going public by writing a book about the child sexual abuse, my adoptive mother launched a vicious, unrelenting smear campaign against me. She had been spreading smears for decades, but quietly and behind my back. Now, she is brazen about doing so. She calls me a liar and mentally ill. She takes every opportunity to spread her slander. That is not a normal response from a mother. She believes that the best defense is an aggressive offense. Her younger sister first made accusations about sexual abuse when I was a teenager. The family crushed her as a result.

As hard as it is to say, I have physical proof of the rape. I have considerable scar tissue internally. Every OB/GYN that I have had has discussed this with me.

The pain never ends. I ask God to explain why. I don't have an answer, just reassurance from Him that someday it will all be clear.

In the meantime, I am now a vocal advocate for victims. We must change how we respond to pedophiles and the profound, lifelong harm they cause.

3

[History of Other Churches and Parachurch Organizations]

The Roman Catholic Church receives most of the headlines regarding child sexual abuse. However, Protestant churches and parachurch organizations also discover pastors, youth leaders, camp counselors, and other personnel who are child molesters. Other religions are not immune to pedophiles taking leadership roles within their organizations. This book offers a scriptural interpretation of the correct response to child sexual abuse within the Church, but the response can be applied to other belief systems as well.

Let's take a look at some more history.

The initial, modern-day reports of child sexual abuse committed by Catholic priests occurred in the 1990s, and the Boston Globe broke the story of 5 Catholic pedophile priests in 2002. Cardinal Bernard Law covered up credible allegations against these 5 pedophiles for years.

When respected media outlets like the Boston Globe published their investigative reports, the issue of clerical child sexual abuse gained recognition. More cases pointed to a widespread coverup by the Roman Catholic Church up and down the hierarchy and across many countries. This led to official investigations by law enforcement in states such as New York, Massachusetts, and Pennsylvania. Canada, the United Kingdom, Ireland, Australia, Belgium, Germany, and the Netherlands all produced their own governmental investigative reports in the 1990s through 2013 that identified thousands of victims of clerical child sexual abuse.

Throughout this period of discovery, the headlines continued to focus largely on the Roman Catholic Church although the abuse was happening in other churches. In addition, several organizations were launched in support of survivors, notably the Survivors Network of those Abused by Priests (SNAP) in the United States, One in Four in the United Kingdom and Ireland, and Broken Rites in Australia.

The increasing public recognition of the Roman Catholic Church scandals made the atmosphere more open for other victims to begin speaking up. It has also led to investigations into Protestant denominations such as the Church of England, the Methodist Church in the UK, and the Anglican Church of Australia.

The lack of investigative studies on clerical child sexual abuse means that the extent of the crimes committed and the number of victims is grossly understated. The damaging, lifelong impact on victims remains obscured.

Mainline Protestant Denominations

Southern Baptists

The Baptist Church is the largest mainline Protestant church in the United States accounting for nearly one-third of all protestants. Since 1998, the Southern Baptist Church has seen approximately

380 church leaders be accused of sexual abuse. They were pastors, youth pastors, Sunday school teachers, deacons, and church volunteers. About 220 were convicted. The number of victims totaled over 700 across 20 years.

In 2021, the Southern Baptist Convention annual meeting set up a task force to address reports of leaders who commit abuse or mishandle allegations of abuse. The church puts forth a zero-tolerance policy and states that "any person in a position of trust or authority who has committed sexual abuse" should be permanently barred from being a pastor or church leader – which still does not follow the apostolic command to put the abuser out of the church.

Messianic

One specific incident happened at Adat Shalom Messianic Church in Dallas, Texas. This incident calls into question the will of the church to implement its zero-tolerance policy. The church allowed Chad Michael Hutchins, a registered sex offender who was convicted for possession of child porn, to teach during services.

In a recording of a phone call, Pastor Robin David Rose defended the decision to allow Hutchins to teach, noting that Hutchins had served his time in prison. He also pointed out that Hutchins' crime had been the possession of pornography, not molesting children. Hutchins was not involved in children's ministry.

Hillsong Church

This megachurch based in Australia was established in 1983 by Brian Houston and his wife, Bobbie. The church is very popular for its worship music with groups like Hillsong United, Hillsong Worship, and Hillsong Young & Free. Until separating from it in 2018, Hillsong was a member of the Australian Christian Churches, which is the Australian branch of the Assemblies of God.

Brian Houston faced charges related to child sex abuse committed by his father, Frank Houston, in the 1970s. An official inquiry into institutional responses to child abuse launched in 2013 heard allegations that the older Houston sexually abused a 7-year-old boy when he came to Australia from New Zealand to preach in 1969 and 1970. Brian Houston was accused of knowing and covering up the allegations against his father. In March 2022, Brian Houston resigned from the megachurch after internal investigations found he had engaged in inappropriate conduct of "serious concern" with two women.

Nondenominational and Non-Christian Groups

The People's Temple lead by Jim Jones forced young girls to strip and perform sexual acts in front of other members.

The Children of God promoted free sex, incest, and child sexual abuse. Rape was accepted as a practice.

The Mormon Church has a history involving church leaders practicing polygamy with children.

The Kingston Group in Utah and Waco Branch Davidians in Texas groomed young girls as sexual partners.

Numerous nondenominational churches have had youth pastors that sexually abused teens in their care. The churches response was to disbelieve the teens and keep the youth pastors -- who were finally caught when they abused others within the church. This is far too common.

Sexual Abuse in the Orthodox Church

There have been many of cases of Orthodox clergy convicted of sexual abuse. However, Orthodox cases receive almost no publicity, unlike Roman Catholic outrages. In one obscure, under-reported case, Fr. Nikolai Stremsky, a priest famous for having the "largest family in Russia" because he had adopted 70 children, was convicted in 2019 of raping and sexually abusing seven children. The Russian Orthodox Church appropriately stripped him of all priestly duties and he was sentenced to 21 years in prison. Unfortunately, this kind of appropriate action is not what is commonly done. It must be done.

In 2020, Asia News reported that several Russian Orthodox bishops were suspended after photos of them were released and circulated on social media. In the photos, the bishops were drunk, naked, and involved in sodomy. Appropriately, without even waiting for a verdict of the ecclesiastical tribunal, the Patriarch suspended the Bishop of Armavir and Labinsk, Ignatijj (Buzin), and the Bishop of Kostomuksha and Kem, Ignatij (Tarasov). However, rather than being sent to prison, the two men were confined in cities far from their dioceses under the supervision of local metropolitans.

The Church has a duty to protect the victims by both excluding the abusers from the Church and working with authorities to prosecute them.

In the U.S., Sally Zakhari accused Fr. Reweiss Aziz Khalil, an Egyptian Coptic Orthodox priest, of sexually abusing her while he was visiting her home when she was 11 or 12. He convinced her mother that it was time for her to begin confession. During her confession she says, "He forcefully kissed me all over my face and in my mouth with his tongue (while he kept on his black tunic)."

Khalil told the girl to never talk about what happened in confession. For the next 17 years, she repeatedly tried to report it to Coptic priests, bishops, and even two popes. She was not taken seriously until she made posts on Facebook and Instagram and her accusations went public. Finally, the Coptic Church appropriately denounced the priest and defrocked him. However, they failed to acknowledge the reason. It is unknown how many other accusations of sexual abuse may have been made against him. Khalil died in 2022.

We need to stop shielding sexual abusers from punishment and the infamy of their deeds.

In one case where a priest was found guilty of sexually assaulting a teen girl, the Greek Orthodox Church was caught attempting to cover it up. Their protocol did not follow the Apostolic command to turn the abuser over to Satan. Instead, they convened a Code of Conduct Council to investigate the complaint, notify the victim, and offer counseling and support services. They encouraged a "mutual resolution" and, if that did not happen, they referred the matter to a canonical court for final determination. If the canonical court decided there was criminal conduct, then the church was required to report that to police authorities. Only then would the archbishop take disciplinary action based on the severity of the complaint. How much time passes from the time the victim reports abuse until the abuse is reported to the police? It ought to be reported immediately.

This Greek Orthodox protocol leaves the victim unprotected from the abuser and having to negotiate with him to reach a "mutual resolution." It does not remove him from the Church where she must still have contact with him. In what cruel fantasyland does a court expect a rape victim or a child who has survived the abuse of a pedophile to come to a "mutual resolution" with her abuser?

A permanent no contact order is appropriate to protect child victims of pedophiles against their abusers. The Church should never place a survivor in a position to have further contact with their abuser.

Some Orthodox Christians believe that there are fewer cases in the Orthodox Church than the Roman Catholic Church, but that may not be the case. Because the Roman Catholic Church is centralized, gathering data has been easier than in Orthodox Churches which, despite professions of apostolic unity, define themselves along clear lines of cultural and geo-political boundaries.

Recent statistics of sexual abuse by Roman Catholic priests indicate between 4% to 7% of them are abusers. No such statistics have been compiled for Protestant or Orthodox churches so there is no way of knowing whether one church or another has more sexual abuse. To their credit, the Roman Catholic Church has compiled statistics.

It is proper to require statistics from the Orthodox Church as it has been to require them from churches who have been more in the public eye because of scandals. If the scandals in the Orthodox Church have been more hidden, it does not mean they are fewer. In fact, cases of sexual abuse in the Orthodox Church seem to be rising.

Some Orthodox Christians have thought that the reason there may be more cases happening in the Orthodox Church now is because the Orthodox Church has lured priests away from the Roman Catholic Church. That is simply not true. Sadly, sexual abuse has occurred in all churches. It is a human problem caused by our human problem of sin.

Some Orthodox believers scan the headlines of scandals in the Roman Catholic Church and think, "That doesn't happen in our Church because our priests are allowed to marry." One Archbishop argued that, "if priests could marry, then the sex scandals could be avoided." This is a dangerous fallacy. Just because someone is Orthodox or goes to church, in no way means they are less dangerous than those outside the Church. In fact, most sex offenders are heterosexual males already in relationships with a woman. Sex crimes are more about power and control than with sex.

In 1991, a layman was accused of sexually abusing at least four children in a Russian Orthodox cathedral in San Francisco, California. His status as a convicted pedophile was believed to have been known to the priest, but was never shared with parishioners. The Church ultimately conceded that the man had abused children, without acknowledging responsibility for his assaults. Because Orthodox churches generally have small congregations, it is harder for victims to remain anonymous when reporting abuse. This makes it harder for them to come forward and report it. When a victim makes a claim of abuse, he or she essentially risks losing their faith community. It does not usually take long to figure out who the accuser is. As in other denominations, the community sadly turns against the survivors and their families. The reasoning is something along the lines of, "Abuse is unknown in the Orthodox churches."

If the abuser is a priest, the problem is compounded. Orthodox clergymen are so highly revered that it is hard for a community to accept that a cleric may have a dark side. The only people who see the dark side of the priest are his victims. When they speak out, they are ostracized. In the Orthodox tradition, the clergy represents God and is the intermediary between God and the people. If the priest abuses you, it is as if God Himself is abusing you. Can you imagine what that does to the faith of the survivors?"

All of the victims in the San Francisco parish, as well as their family members, lost their faith in the Church because of the way that case was handled by Orthodox officials." How tragic!

We must stop blaming victims for the crimes of their abusers. We can and must do better.

The Greek Orthodox Church published its policy on sexual misconduct in 2000, and operates a confidential hotline (212) 774-0332 to answer questions about its policy and to accept complaints about sexual misconduct by clergy.

The Orthodox Church in America (OCA) now requires all adults to take a training course "Stewards of Children." The Holy Synod of Bishops of the OCA approved a revised Policy, Standards, and Procedures on Sexual Misconduct in 2013. "This policy is now in force in the Church. It is the goal of the entire Church to provide a safe and healthy environment for all of the faithful of the Orthodox

Church in America. The Church laments the sin of sexual misconduct, and will not tolerate sexual misconduct by its clergy or any layperson."

Sexual abuse occurs in every church and every kind of business. Abusers gravitate toward jobs where they have easy access to children. To protect the children and also limit liability to the Church from million-dollar lawsuits, many churches have instituted policies that (1) prohibit any clergy from interacting alone with a child and (2) requiring extensive background checks, including fingerprints, of those wishing to work with children. Such policies might protect the Orthodox Church, as well as providing better protection for children, by identifying known sexual predators. Some insurance companies are refusing to insure churches that do not have such policies.

It is up to each and every member of the church to be vigilant and report sexual abuse within the Church to both church authorities and to the local police.

4

[Nancy's Story]

I was about nine years old. My parents had divorced and my mother had placed me in the care of an aunt while my mom went to school to learn a trade. My cousins and I were playing outside in a long trench that had been dug for a septic tank. At the end of the trench, was the big hole for the septic tank. It was covered over with a corrugated tin roof.

My teenage cousin, Donnie, was six years older than me. The boys led all of us through the trench and into the "cave" of the septic tank. It was dark and spooky. I could hear the other children laughing, giggling, and having fun. Donnie was tickling me when suddenly he was holding me so tight it hurt and he reached his hand inside my panties. He groped me and stuck his finger inside of me. It hurt. I was screaming, but he wouldn't stop. It was too dark for the other children to see what he was doing.

I kept screaming louder and louder. A hand reached down into the opening of the cave and his mother pulled Donnie out. I crawled out behind him, sobbing. His mother twisted his ear and led him into the house. She didn't look back, comfort me, or ask what happened.

I decided I would tell my mom. But when my mom arrived for dinner that night, I was sitting by my uncle, the town sheriff. He was wearing his gun. Donnie was leering at me from across the table. I felt too intimidated to talk to Mom.

Later, my mom and I moved to an apartment house. The landlord was an old family friend she had known since childhood. We all called him Uncle Ernie. Everyone said he loved the children and he often played with us. He liked to give the girls piggyback rides. One day, he reached up under my panties as I was riding on his back. He was fondling me and trying to put his finger inside me. I leaped off his back, pushed him away and said loudly, "I'll tell my mom!"

I ran into my apartment. That evening, as my mom was getting home from work, I heard a commotion outside. I went out onto the second-floor balcony and saw that my beloved cat had been run over by a car. Uncle Ernie was bending over its body, looking sternly up at me. I was afraid of him, so I didn't tell my mom what he had done. I could not have put it into words as a child, but I was terrified he would kill me or that I would lose my home and Mom if I told. That thought of losing my mom caused fear of abandonment that created major problems for me as an adult.

Once, when Mom had to be out of town, she left me under the care of Uncle Ernie for a week. He lived in another apartment with his wife, but had a key to our apartment. I can't remember anything about that week. I know I had a bed in my bedroom, but there is only a blank space where the bed was in my memory. I can remember the rest of the room, the furniture, the closet, but I can't remember the bed. I don't want to remember.

I didn't tell Mom about cousin Donnie or Uncle Ernie until I was 28 years old when Uncle Ernie died. She did not believe me.

Nothing ever happened to my two sexual abusers. They remained in the family. I had flashbacks and nightmares well into middle age.

My Mom did not want anyone to think she had been a bad mother, I suppose. So, she began telling family members that I was crazy and a liar. She was a great storyteller, very entertaining, and people didn't know that many of her stories were false.

I married at 16 after a date rape on my very first car date. I had no boundaries and did not feel I could say no. I knew I wasn't a virgin after that and thought I had no choice but to marry him, that no one would ever want me. I had five children with this abusive man. After a divorce, I had a devastating depression. It took the doctors years to get my medications right. During those years, my behavior caused so much sorrow for my children. I can never make that up to them. I became homeless, suicidal, and unemployable. I had zero family support during that time.

My mother continued to deny my childhood sexual abuse. I was shut out of family events, not allowed to see my grandchildren, called a crazy liar. I always felt like I was on a witness stand being cross examined when I talked to them. My brother said my family's behavior was like a shark feeding frenzy. Eventually, some family members stopped speaking to me entirely. I have a good psychiatrist and have been stable on medication for many years now. But the devastation caused by child sexual abuse has been extremely painful and long lasting. It's been 44 years since I told my mom, 68 years since the abuse happened; the pain never goes away.

5

[Sexual Abuse: A Guide for Church Leaders]

All sexual abuse committed by church leaders is a form of incest because we all are children of God. We are brothers and sisters of one another and of Christ, as is plain in the Bible:

"But to all who did receive him, who believed in his name, he gave the right to become children of God, who were born, not of blood nor of the will of the flesh nor of the will of man, but of God." John 1:12-13

"See what kind of love the Father has given to us, that we should be called children of God; and so we are." 1 John 3:1

"So then you are no longer strangers and aliens, but you are fellow citizens with the saints and members of the household of God," Ephesians 2:19

What is the right response from the Church to child sexual abuse and incest? What do the scriptures say?

The pastor is very often the first person an incest victim turns to for help, and too often pastors are unprepared to do that. Almost nothing is taught about incest in seminary or Bible college. It is our hope that this book can serve as a guide for pastors and church members when they are confronted with the problem of incest in the church.

A victim asks, "Who rises up for me against the wicked? Who stands up for me against evildoers?" (Psalm 94:16)

Church, stand up!

Incest in the Church: The Gravity of the Situation

A man who has been a believer, and then commits incest, is like Esau who sold his birthright for a pot of soup. That was a very poor trade because his birthright included two-thirds of his father's estate. He is thus said to have despised his birthright. He thought more of his base desire than for his precious birthright. (Genesis 25:29-34)

The incest abuser is unholy, blasphemous, obscene, disrespectful, irreverent, and profane. The author of Hebrews warns, "See to it that no one fails to obtain the grace of God; . . . that no one is sexually immoral or unholy like Esau who sold his birthright for a single meal. For you know that afterward when he desired to inherit the blessing, he was rejected for he found no place to repent, though he sought it with tears." (Hebrews 12:15-17)

"See to it" in this verse is a command, not a suggestion. It is a command addressed to all of us, not merely pastors, priests, deacons, or elders. We are all, as a body, to "see to it" that the Apostle's command regarding the incest abuser is carried out.

The man who has done this has despised and forfeited the great and precious inheritance that he formerly had among the saints, just as Reuben forfeited his birthright for incest in 1 Chronicles 5:1. ". . . for you can be sure of this, that everyone who is sexually immoral or impure ... has no inheritance of the kingdom of Christ and God." (Ephesians 5:5) He despised His inheritance in Christ to indulge in depravity. It would have been better for him to have never known the way of righteousness than, after knowing it, to turn back. (2 Peter 2:21) He has turned back, like a dog, to his own vomit and like a sow who, after washing herself, returns to wallow in the mire. (2 Peter 2:22) He exchanged eternal glory for the momentary gratification of the flesh.

The Apostle Paul knew well the laws regarding incest that are recorded in Leviticus 18 and that the required punishment was clear. After listing the incest prohibitions, the Bible says, "For everyone who does any of these abominations, the persons who do them shall be cut off from among their people." (Leviticus 18:29 ESV) The NCB translation stresses the mandatory nature of the punishment, "Everyone who does any of these detestable things—such persons must be cut off from their people." (Leviticus 18:29 NCB).

The Church's Duty to Remove the Incest Abuser from the Church

In 1 Corinthians 5:1-12, Paul sternly commands the church to remove the man who commits incest from the church, to "purge the evil person from among you." (1 Corinthians 5:3) The church is to have no fellowship with this man, but rather expose him (for it is shameful to even speak of his sin -- a sin that not even pagans accept). (Ephesians 5:11-12)

To allow a Christian man doing this evil to continue to be part of the church not only pollutes the church, it puts the evildoer in danger of God's wrath, which is terrible to contemplate. Being put out of the church with the hope of being saved in the Day of the Lord is more merciful -- even to him -- than allowing an incest abuser to remain.

Before he traveled to Corinth, Paul incredulously wrote, "It is actually reported that there is sexual immorality among you, and of a kind that is not tolerated even among pagans, for a man has his father's wife. And you are arrogant! Ought you not to mourn? Let him who has done this be put away from you." (1 Corinthians 5:2)

The Reason for Putting the Incest Abuser Out of the Church

We put the abuser out of the church in obedience to the command of the Apostle Paul. When we submit to the command of an Apostle or prophet, we are submitting to the Lord. In 1 Kings 20, the prophet Isaiah condemned Ahab because Ahab did not obey the prophet, saying, "Because you have not obeyed the Lord . . ." His punishment was death. Again, in chapter 13, when a man did not obey a prophet, the prophet told him, "You have defiled the Word of the Lord and have not kept the command the Lord your God gave you." (1 Kings 13:21) His punishment was to be torn apart by a lion. It is no small thing to ignore the command of an Apostle.

The Church is to submit to Christ in all things so that He, Jesus, . . . might sanctify her by the washing of water with the Word, so that He might present the Church to Himself in splendor without spot or wrinkle or any such thing, so that she might be holy and without blemish. (Ephesians 5:24, 26-27) * *

We Put the Abuser Out Because It Is the One Thing Necessary to Do

An incest abuser is a liar, a con man, a manipulator. When caught, he may seek a quick and easy "repentance" and family reunion, but do not be deceived. He is accustomed to lying and pretense. He is a master at manipulating to satisfy his own desires. The Apostle tells the church to do one thing -- and one thing only -- put the man out of the church. The only question is, will you obey or not?

The Time for Putting the Incest Abuser Out of the Church

Not only was the Corinthian church tolerating an incest abuser in their assembly, they were arrogant, proud, and thinking highly of themselves. Pride and arrogance are earmarks of modern churches who tolerate the most egregious kinds of sexual sin, but the Apostle Paul pronounced judgment against the incest abuser, even before he arrived at the church. Paul said, "For though absent in body, I am present in spirit, and as if present, I have already pronounced judgment on the one who did such a thing." (1 Corinthians 5:3)

There is to be no delay in pronouncing judgment against incest abusers, no scheduling of committee meetings to discuss the problem, no bringing the incest abuser before the elders, no counseling sessions to encourage him to confess and repent and be forgiven. Paul pronounced judgment as soon as he was aware of it; the Church must do likewise.

The Mercy of Putting the Incest Abuser Out of the Church

The power and goodness that generates all life is dangerous if you draw close to it while you are doing evil. You must be pure to come into the presence of God. A believer practicing evil is in great danger. For his own safety, he must be removed.

There is greater mercy under the New Covenant than there was for those who brought defilement before the Mercy Seat in the Tabernacle; putting an evil man out of the church with the hope that he might be saved is a more merciful penalty than being struck dead.

Unlike the punishment for incest under the Law, which was death by stoning of both parties, it was clear that Paul did not judge the woman; he pronounced judgment on the man only and gave instructions to the Church on how to handle it. He said, "When you are assembled, in the name of the Lord Jesus Christ, and my spirit is present, with the power of our Lord Jesus, you are to deliver this man to Satan for the destruction of the flesh, so that his spirit may be saved in the Day of the Lord." (1 Corinthians 5:4-5) In the New

Testament, it is the abuser, not the victim, who is to be excluded, and the victim may of either gender.

The incest abuser is to be put out of the church to be buffeted by Satan, so that, by Satan's buffeting, he might be saved in the day of the Lord. Putting him out is a mercy and benefit to him. Although it is true that he will suffer sharp, repeated blows from Satan; be battered by the winds and the waves that are controlled by the prince of the power of the air; be attacked; be knocked off course; suffer misfortunes and difficulties; and be afflicted and harmed repeatedly over a long period of time -- this is the dire condition of one who brings evil into the church and disgraces the Bride of Christ.

This is the Punishment for Incest Abusers within the Church

The book of Hebrews is written to "us," that is, to Christian believers, "We must pay more careful attention, therefore, to what we have heard, so that we do not drift away. For if the message spoken by angels was binding, and every violation and disobedience received its just punishment, how shall we live if we neglect so great a salvation?" (Hebrews 1:1-3a) It is the responsibility of the entire church to see that justice is done when sexual abuse has happened.

Does this sound harsh? Under the law, the man would have been stoned to death and so would the woman. "If a man is found lying with the wife of another man, both of them shall die, the man who lay with the woman, and the woman. So shall you purge the evil from Israel." (Deuteronomy 21:22) The harshness of the Law is tempered by grace and mercy in the New Testament.

Contrary to modern feminist teaching, the outworking of the gospel always brings about greater respect, compassion, and mercy for women. In the case of incest in the Corinthian Church, the punishment may have been directed only at the man for two reasons: 1) the woman may not have been a follower of Christ, or 2) the Apostle recognized the greater responsibility of the man; the woman had less power both by physical strength and society's financial and social restrictions placed upon her, and therefore less accountability. The Bible is silent on which one was true in this case, and where the Bible is silent, we will be also.

The Incest Abuser Is to Be Put Out of the Church to Preserve Holiness

Holiness describes how God is the creative force behind the whole universe. He is utterly unique and sovereign over all. He is Other. He is set apart. He is holy

Isaiah prophesied of our day, saying, "And a highway shall be there, and it shall be called the way of holiness; the unclean shall not pass over it, but it shall be for those: the wayfarers, though fools, shall not err therein." (Isaiah 35:8) Yes, we are fools for Christ, wayfaring strangers in this world of woe, but we do not err when we put away evil from the Church.

We are to put the incest abuser out to preserve holiness in the Church. Our worship in the assembly must be maintained with holiness and reverential fear, "O worship the Lord in the beauty of holiness; fear before Him all the earth." (Psalm 96:9) We are to rejoice in holiness, "Rejoice in the Lord, ye righteous, and give thanks at the remembrance of His holiness." (Psalm 97:12) "For God has not called us for impurity, but for holiness." (1 Thessalonians 4:7)

We Put Out the Incest Abuser to Separate Ourselves

Regardless, of his outward protestation, the incest abuser is even worse than a pagan; because he claimed to be a believer and was part of the Christian assembly, he is worse than an unbeliever. You do not rape a child or a woman and claim to believe in God. You do not have sex with a close family member and claim to be a Christian. That is an outrage! You do not remain in the church if you do such things.

We have been bought with the precious blood of Christ, like that of a lamb without blemish or spot and it is our duty to keep ourselves and the assembly pure. The Church is the bride of Christ. There ought to be no spot, no blemish, no evil in the Church. (1 Peter 1:19) That would be like making the Bride of Christ wear a white dress with black ink spotting it. The evil must be purged from the Church, which is the Bride of Christ.

"Do not be unequally yoked with unbelievers for what partnership has righteousness with lawlessness? Or what fellowship has light with darkness? What accord has Christ with Belial? Or what portion does a believer have with an unbeliever?" (2 Corinthians 7:1) ". . . separate from them, says the Lord, and touch no unclean thing; then I will welcome you, and I will be a father to you, and you shall be sons and daughters to me,' says the Lord Almighty." (2 Corinthians 6:17-18)

Israel was commanded to purge evil from its midst by the death penalty. Holiness in the presence of God was an absolute requirement. The Church is to purge evil from its midst by putting sexual abusers out of the Church.

No one was permitted to defile the Tabernacle. When the sons of Aaron, Nadab and Abihu, approached the holy place and offered strange fire that the Lord had not commanded, they died. (Leviticus 16:1) The Day of Atonement ritual was then necessary to atone for the defilement of the Tabernacle. God told Moses, "Tell Aaron your brother not to come in at any time into the Holy Place inside the veil, before the mercy seat that is on the ark, so that he may not die."

We, the body of Christ, are God's Tabernacle; we are not to permit the presence of evil that defiles the Church nor that places a brother in danger of being struck dead by God's wrath. Incest abuse is that serious.

Consider the swiftness and permanence of God's wrath and His just punishment in the case of Ananias and Sapphira in Acts 5. They had stolen from the church and lied to the Holy Spirit. God immediately struck them dead. "And great fear came upon the whole church and upon all who heard of these things."

We Put Out the Incest Abuser Regardless of His Position

The biblical remedy is not to call an incest abuser to repentance, but to put him out. This was true in both the Old and New testaments.

Regardless of a man's position in the church, an incest abuser is to be put out of the church. Is he a deacon? Put him out. Is he a pastor? Put him out. Does he contribute large sums to the church? Put him out.

Regardless of a man's position in the family, he is to be put out of the family.

The incest abuser rightfully loses his place in both the church and the family; no one does this to him; he did it to himself. Reuben was Jacob's firstborn, but he lost his birthright when he defiled his father's marriage bed. "Reuben, the firstborn of Israel for he was the firstborn, but when he defiled his father's bed, his birthright was given to the sons of Joseph. For this reason, he could not be listed in the genealogy according to his birthright." (1 Chronicles 5:1 NCB

We Honor Christ by Obeying the Apostle's Command

"You were bought with a price" (1 Corinthians 7:23 ESV) When we disobey the Apostle and offer a quick and easy repentance to an incest abuser, we cheapen the great sacrifice that was required to purchase our salvation. Of course, the man says he is sorry! He is sorry he got caught and, being an experienced liar and manipulator, he is going to blubber his way to whatever he thinks you want to hear that will permit his life to go on as normal. That is exactly what the church must not allow him to do.

His life ought to never be the same. We put the incest abuser out of the church so the victim(s) can heal. Restoring the victim's life to shalom ought to be the main concern of the church. Shalom is often translated from the Hebrew as "peace." But it means so much more. When a loss or injury occurred among the ancient Hebrews, the victim was considered lacking, incomplete. Shalom means "to make it good, "to surely pay," "to make whole." The offender was required to surely pay for his offense. The ancient Hebrew meaning of shalom implied a sense of good health, blessing, and completeness in body and soul for the victim of theft or bodily injury.

Although the incest abuser will suffer, he is nevertheless to be put out of the church. Doing so respects and supports the victim of sexual abuse. It allows healing to begin, which cannot happen in the presence of his or her abuser.

We Put the Abuser Out So That Others Shall Hear and Fear

Why is there so much sexual immorality in today's churches? One reason is that the churches tolerate it. Tolerance is held out as a virtue and the clear commands of scripture are ignored.

Under the law, evil was to be purged from their midst so that all the people shall hear and fear and not act presumptuously again." (Deuteronomy 17:12) "And the rest shall hear and fear, and shall never again commit any such evil among you." (Deuteronomy 19:19) From this we learn that the purpose in excluding someone from the assembly is not merely to punish the one who commits evil, but that others might learn and fear to act in such an evil manner. (Deuteronomy 17:12)

1 Corinthians chapter 10 is a warning to all believers to take heed lest they be overthrown as were the Israelites, "For I do not want you to be unaware brothers, that our fathers were all under the cloud, and all passed through the sea, and all were baptized into Moses in the cloud and in the sea, and all ate the same spiritual

food, and all drank the same spiritual drink. For they drank from the spiritual Rock that followed them, and the Rock was Christ. Nevertheless, with most of them God was not pleased, for they were overthrown in the wilderness." (1 Corinthians 10:1-5 ESV).

The situation of a church member who has committed incest abuse is similar for he has walked with us, been baptized, ate and drank at the table of the Lord with us. "There is one body and one Spirit--just as you were called to the one hope that belongs to your call--one Lord, one faith, one baptism, one God and Father of all, who is over all and through all, and in all." (Ephesians 4:4-5)

"You cannot drink the cup of the Lord and the cup of demons. You cannot partake of the table of the Lord and the table of demons." (1 Corinthians 10:21) Incest and sexual abuse are demonic.

"Now these things took place as examples for us, that we might not desire evil as they did. (1 Corinthians 10:6 ESV)

Both justice and punishment act as a deterrent to sexual immorality. This was true in Acts 5 when great fear came upon the whole church.

It is appropriate to put out an incest abuser from the assembly so that others will conduct themselves with holiness and fear. Believers are called to be holy. "As obedient children, do not be conformed to the passions of your former ignorance, but as He who called you is holy, you also be holy in all your conduct, since it is written, 'You shall be holy as I am holy.' . . . conduct yourselves with fear . . ." (1 Peter 1:15)

Setting Priorities in Cases of Incest

Purging evil from the church and restoring shalom to the victim ought to be the main concerns of the church, not demanding confession, repentance and forgiveness from the victim of sexual abuse, as is generally done. This places the burden of restoration on the victim; burdens ought to be placed only on the abuser. Forgiveness is important; it is Christ's command to forgive but forgiveness is not for us to command others to do. Forgiveness is something a survivor of sexual abuse may choose to do after justice and healing have been done; forgiveness is for the survivor, not the abuser. It enables survivors to have peace in their own souls.

The priorities of the church must be:

- To obey the command of the Apostle (and thereby the command of the Lord) to remove the sexual abuser from the church.
- To see that justice is done for the victim(s).
- To see to it that church members conduct themselves with holiness and fear.
- To correct those who grumble.

**Footnote: Pay attention to the words that indicate Paul's main purpose in this passage was to command that an incest abuser be put out of the church. He speaks of normal family and social relationships. Ephesians 5:25 is urging children to obey their fathers, slaves to obey their masters, and husbands to love their wives. It is Christ Himself who presents the Church in splendor. The preface regarding the order of society and family is all in preparation for Paul's main message about maintaining purity in the Church, which was the problem at Corinth.

We Put the Abuser Out to Restore Normal Family Relationships

You can think of the family as a delicate mobile hung over a baby's crib. When you touch one part of the mobile, all the other parts start moving. Incest touches everyone in the family in different, usually unhealthy ways.

One of the ways incest affects the family in a similar way is that, when an abuser is allowed to remain in the family, family members take sides. There is a strong desire for things to "be normal" again. Some family members deny the abuse happens. Others minimize it. Many insist the victim should forgive so they can enjoy family holidays together.

These attitudes put undue pressure on the victim to:

- Forgive before justice is done
- Retract her accusation
- Deny her rightful feelings of discomfort around the abuser

In this manner, blame for family division and discomfort is put on the victim. The responsibility to make the family whole is placed on her. She is shamed and cut off from family members who refused to put out the abuser. It doesn't matter whether she becomes a prostitute or a Sunday School teacher; she will be shamed, blamed, and often outcast. The damage to the victim in such cases is severe and lifelong.

People want the family mobile to stop being out of whack. They would rather minimize the abuse or pretend it never happened than deal with the consequences of real trauma. However, the person who must feel OK again is the victim; she is the one who needs healing. The other family members must adjust to the division in the family caused by the abuser. He and he alone is to blame for it.

A Pastoral Response to Incest

After incest abuse, some pastors will wrongly recommend:

- Counseling for both the family and the victim (with the goal of reuniting the family)

THE CHURCH OF GOMORRAH | 39

- Letting the Word of God convict the abuser (Would we recommend that to a murderer without seeking justice?)
- Letting God help him overcome his "problem"
- That the abuser receives Jesus Christ as a way of solving the problem
- Reconciling the family with the abuser after he has prayed a prayer to receive Christ

A pastor may wrongly:

- Fail to notify the police.
- Assure the family that the abuser has confessed his behavior as sin and now must be allowed back into the family.
- Recommend that the family leave it up to God to correct and deliver the abuser.
- Encourage prayer as a means of restoring the family's broken cords of relationship.
- Tell the victim to forgive and forget, so she won't tear the family apart.
- Tell the woman that she is not free to divorce the incest abuser (scripturally, she is).
- Blame the victim if she acts out in negative ways or at some point became a willing participant in the sexual acts (this is normal behavior for victims of sexual abuse.)
- Recommend that the incest abuser stay in close contact with the pastor (of the victim's own church) and with other members of her family

All of these are aimed at restoration of the abuser and do nothing to bring about justice or protect the victim. None of these obey the clear instruction of the Bible to put the abuser out.

"Where is the one who is wise? . . . Has God not made foolish the wisdom of this world?" (1 Corinthians 1:20 ESV)

What is important to stress is that everything we do as a church and as a family must put the healing of the victim before everything else. She is the one who has been damaged the most, and the family must rally around her and stand united. By his own actions, he has forfeited his right to be part of the family.

The Apostle Paul knew that none of these things that pastors try would bring about justice and healing; he did not mess around. He put the incest abuser out of the Corinthian Church immediately. That is what heals the victim. That it is the model for churches and families. If people want to be contentious, let them argue with the Apostle. They do so to their own condemnation.

What Happens When the Abuser Remains?

The proper response of the family and of the church family is to put the man out, to protect the victim, and to firmly be united in standing with her. She ought not be the one to have to stay away from church or family gatherings because of discomfort around the abuser; if anyone is uncomfortable, it ought to be the abuser. But often churches and families will immediately or gradually allow the abuser back in.

The Bible says, "Take your evil deeds out of my sight! Stop doing wrong, learn to do right! Seek justice, encourage the oppressed." (Isaiah 1:16)

When people continue their relationships with the incest abuser, it robs the victim of peace and puts the burden on her to forgive and forget in order to make things right. It is disrespectful of the entire church and family who have been damaged by the sin of incest. It may make some members feel better to forgive and forget; that does not make it the right thing to do. And, most important of all, it disobeys the Lord who spoke by the Apostle Paul.

People do this for their own selfish peace, so they do not have to deal with the gross abuse that has happened (they can pretend everything is ok; it was a long time ago; she ought to get over it; all she has to do is forgive him) It is not up to the survivor to put things right; putting things right means to exclude the incest abuser from the church and from the family. Period. By his own actions, he has lost his right to be part of the family of God and of her own family.

Families who put such burdens on the victim(s) eventually shame and blame the victim rather than the abuser.

For most families, incest abuse requires counseling -- privately for the survivor, and separately for family members. It does not include counseling for the abuser with the survivor or her family; he is out of the family. Period.

Keeping an abuser within the family is extremely damaging to a victim and to the entire family system. Sometimes the abuse goes on for generations because it is not dealt with swiftly and severely, as it deserves to be.

Consider the case of a father who violently beats and sexually abuses several of his daughters. The mother stays because she has five other children, is not educated, and believes (wrongly!) that she can't survive without him. What happens? The daughters learn helplessness from their mother's example. They normalize incest and are conditioned to believe that incest is something they must live with.

In the next generation, one of the abused daughters has two daughters. They are both sexually abused by their stepfather from the time they are toddlers until they are in their teens. The mother is aware of the abuse, but stays because of her learned helplessness.

In the next generation, the daughters are forced to forgive and the abuser is kept in the family, celebrates Christmas and other holidays with them, gives the mother and daughters money to keep them dependent on him and to silence them. They comply and keep the family secret. One daughter becomes a drunk and the other becomes a drug addict, prostitute, mentally ill, and a violent criminal. But Grandpa, the incest abuser, is still opening gifts and sitting at the family table on Christmas. If a survivor sits through such family gatherings, she is forced to swallow her pain with every bite. Her pain is never healed and produces many other problems for her.

When an abuser is not cast out, there is no justice for the survivors of incest. There is no healing for them and only a cover-up, not true healing, for the family. It continues on generation after generation. This is what happens when survivors are told to quickly "forgive" -- as if THAT is the solution to incest! The Apostle Paul knew better.

Consider what happens when a woman reveals incest to her mother. The mother is shocked and immediately feels guilt and shame that she did not know what was happening, or did not protect her child. She thinks that she will be considered a "bad mother" for not helping her child when she was little. What does she do? She denies that the abuse happened, denies it even to herself. She calls her daughter crazy and a liar, and slanders her to family, friends, and the church. The family's flying monkeys gather round to support the mother and castigate the victim. The victim becomes the family scapegoat; whenever there is a problem in the family, no matter the cause, it is seen as the victim's fault and she is shut out like the scapegoat in scripture who had all the sins of the community put upon it and was sent out into the desert to die alone. (Leviticus 16:20-21)

Imagine the pain of being the scapegoat! It is justice to shame, blame, and cast out the incest abuser. It is not justice to do that to the survivor of his crime.

The consequences of untreated sexual abuse are huge and they affect families for generations. It is vital that families and churches honestly face the problem of incest and cast out the abuser. The Apostle Paul, in the power of the Holy Spirit, commanded it. To obey him is to obey the Lord.

What the church must offer is real healing and that comes by obeying the Word of God. Does this cause suffering for the abuser? Yes, most assuredly. God takes corrective action because of sin and disobedience. He teaches us to respond to problems in a godly way. Even Jesus "learned obedience by the things which He suffered." (Hebrews 5:8)

The Church is in a position to bring about healing, and the first step is to take a firm stand against an incest abuser and cast him out. Families, however painful it may be, must do the same.

But Didn't Christ Teach Us to Forgive?

Yes, and some think the Church should forgive sexual abusers and let them back into the fellowship of the Church. After all, didn't Paul tell the Church in 2 Corinthians to forgive the incest abuser and let him back in?" They base their question on Paul's words, "But if anyone has caused grief, he has not grieved me, but all of you to some extent – not to be too severe. This punishment which was inflicted by the majority is sufficient for such a man, so that on the contrary, you ought rather to forgive and comfort him lest perhaps such a one be swallowed up with too much sorrow. Therefore, I urge you to reaffirm your love for him." (2 Corinthians 2:5-8)

Some theologians have mistakenly thought that this refers to the incest abuser in 1 Corinthians 5. However, there is no basis to believe that. There is evidence that other letters were sent to the Corinthian Church in between what we know today as 1st and 2nd Corinthians. The man who received "punishment which was inflicted by the majority" may have been identified in those letters that did not become part of the biblical canon. He may have been punished for any number of things that caused pain to the church: theft, gossip, slander, lying, and so on. Who "caused pain" is not specified in 2 Corinthians and it is wrong to "fill-in-the-blank" with the incest abuser.

We simply do not know who "caused pain" but we can be confident it was not the sexual abuser for several reasons:

- The mere "majority" mentioned in 2 Corinthians does not refer to the entire Church, gathered together, along with Paul's spirit, and our Lord Jesus Christ, and so cannot be referring to the incest abuser who was cast out by the entire Church, along with Paul, and our Lord Jesus Christ.
- Another reason it does not refer to the incest abuser was that Paul told the Church to "deliver such a one to Satan for the destruction of the flesh." This is far from the same wording in 2 Corinthians of a mere punishment by the Church. Destruction means destruction. You don't restore one whose flesh has been destroyed. One whose flesh is destroyed is dead – dead to the church and eventually dead in his body. His only hope is to be saved on the Day of the Lord.
- Finally, the incest abuser was to be put out "until the Day of the Lord" which is at the end of time, not to be welcomed back into the Church. Extending forgiveness to other kinds of offenders in no way negates the Apostle's order to put sexual abusers out of the Church.

6

Nicole's Story

[Nicole's Story]

The sexual abuse began with a neighbor, Jerry, who babysat me when I was four years old. When I fell down, he bandaged my knees and then proceeded to slide his hands up my legs to fondle me. It progressed from there.

My Dad was often gone at work, and when he was home my parents were fighting. When my dad hit her, she was laying on the floor beat up so bad she couldn't move. I grabbed my sister and we ran to the only house where there were people. Jerry was there. Ultimately, my parents divorced and my abuser married my mother.

He caused a semi-truck accident in which his best friend was killed and he was seriously injured. He received a very large insurance settlement. We moved from a small house in the poor part of town to a beautiful large home with new furniture. We children all had our own bedrooms. Jerry appeared to be the hero who rescued my mom and her little girls. When my mom went to school and worked, he stayed home and babysat. He was always laid off work so he had plenty of time to abuse me. When I was six or seven, I was very sick and had to stay home from school, and he had free access to abuse me even more.

At about the age of 10 to 12, I realized that if I willingly participated, I could get stuff from him. The sexual abuse continued till I was fourteen. I became desensitized to sex as a loving thing, and it turned into an opportunity to get the things I wanted. This planted the seed in my mind for protecting the abuser and thinking it was okay to do sexual favors in return for freedom and money and to survive.

When I had my first boyfriend at 14, the young man realized what was going on, and he said, "It's wrong. Get help." The dynamic between my abuser and I changed. It became uncomfortable and disgusting. It was not worth his presents. I started to realize it wasn't right.

My Mom was preoccupied with her career, her hair, her clothes, and a secret boyfriend. I didn't think she knew what was going on. I found out later that she did.

My aunt's husband came on the weekends and took me and my sister to my Dad's Grandma, but Jerry would not let us go unless he knew my mom was going to be gone. On weekends when we could go to grandma's, my aunt would take us to church. On those weekends, he didn't have the chance to abuse me.

When I was 14, I finally told my mom's sister about the sexual abuse, and my mother left him. She took us to live with her various sisters. We were moving around quite a bit. I had been a straight A student and a cheerleader. But now there was no place for me to study. My grades dropped. I lost my position in my social life at school. I didn't have clean clothes. I couldn't do my hair in the morning.

I started hanging around with the wrong friends in the neighborhood where we were living. Mom was still working and we children were running around. We hung out with older boys who had alcohol and pot. All that replaced my private bedroom and desk where I had studied. I lost the ability to learn the things I ought to have been learning as a teenager.

My family was so displaced and impoverished that my mom thought it better to go back to the abuser. Instead of protecting me from him, my mother said it was my decision. The burden of the decision was placed on me, a child, rather than on the parent who should have protected her child.

In the one and only counseling session we had, the abuser was present, and it was made clear to me that it was solely my decision to go back. It was up to me to make sure that all of us had a nice home. If I didn't go back, I was told I would be keeping my mother homeless and in poverty. My Mom's entire extended family thought it was best for my mother. My Dad was out of the picture, having moved out of state. The stability of the extended family depended on me, a young teen. I absolutely could not go against a family of 30. Rather than my mother taking responsibility for the family's peace and welfare, it was dumped on me. So, we went back.

No adult ever told me that what he was doing was wrong; they said what I was doing was wrong. Nobody said this is against the law. They said you are wrong to keep your family in poverty, and make the rest of the family take care of you and your mom and sister.

When we went back, the abuse started again and it became violent. Before I told, he acted like he was teaching me about sex. When I went back, he started abusing me brutally. Then he started giving me alcohol so I would be more submissive.

So, I became attracted to dark and violent friends. I continued drinking and running the streets with a bad crowd. That's when the family started blaming me, shaming me, and pushing me out, saying that all of this was my fault. The incest abuser was still held out to be the hero, trying to make a good life for us.

I did whatever I could to get out. I ran away with a known killer who also killed my best friend. He killed other people along the way while we were fleeing from police.

After my best friend was murdered, and I had run away with the killer, he shot another man dead who had picked us up hitchhiking. He took his car and we continued running. I got away from the killer in another state and called home. I was brought back and he was caught and arrested. I was placed in a juvenile detention facility. I later testified against him, and he was sentenced to life in prison.

My aunt had also moved out of state, but she visited at just that time. She confronted my mother and asked,

"Did you know?"

"My mother said, "yes."

My Aunt said, "WHY did you stay with him?"

My mother replied, "Well, you know, I needed the house and the insurance."

My Aunt's brother-in-law was the Chief of Police. She asked him if he knew. He said, "We suspected." My aunt was horrified and said, "WHY didn't you tell us? We could have done something."

After the murder trial, I moved to the state where my dad was, got pregnant, and was sent to an institution. I was still in the girl's reform school when my baby was born, shortly before my 18th birthday. They took my baby, and put her up for adoption.

The family ran my new boyfriend off. He was my baby's father who was going to marry me. They took away my chance for my own family. I was never able to have another baby.

I was too damaged to ever have a successful relationship again.

Eventually my mother did divorce my abuser, however she went back to him -- even after she knew about the sexual abuse.

Her comfort was more important than my life, and 40 years later, it still is.

As a sexually abused child, I am constantly yearning for my family's love. That little girl side of me still needs my mother and father. My father is dead. Every time I try to seek my mother's love and do something good, she and her family smash me down again.

I am still involved with my mother's family who blamed, shamed, and exiled me. All my hopes and dreams were shattered. I am finally in touch with the daughter who was adopted out, but my birth family got to know her and poisoned her mind against me.

I still talk to my mother's family on the phone. My daughter is invited to family reunions, but not me. Still today, the reason they claim they shut me out is that I am an alcoholic and a drug abuser, but they don't blame the man who abused me. My mother, still, 40 years later, is getting money from him. He writes "child support" on the check.

The only ones who ever said the abuse was wrong were my dad's only sister and my friend Tracy. My own sister insists that I stay in contact with my mom because she thinks it's the right thing to do and it would be best to pretend it never happened. She says, "it's a long time ago." For me, it's still happening today. My life is still disturbed today. That day has never gone away for me. My sister became an alcoholic herself; maybe that's how she deals with the pain.

I was shunned by my mother's family and went into the criminal subculture to hide from the pain. I hid from all of them, except my sister. They didn't know where I was. I thought they couldn't hurt me anymore. I sold my body because that was what I did for my abuser.

All these years later, I am still yearning for love and acceptance from my mother's family and am still in my addiction, unable to have any type of normal relationship with a man. Inwardly, I am still 14 with a 14-year-old's skills, limited in my ability to cope with the world.

7

[Believe The Children]

What happens when a young child discloses that he or she is being sexually abused? If she has made the disclosure to a "mandatory reporter" like a teacher, Child Protective Services and law enforcement become involved. The alleged perpetrator may be arrested, although he is innocent until proven guilty as a matter of law. If he is a family member, he returns to the family until trial unless he is held in prison without bail or a restraining order is issued. If he is a priest or pastor at the family's church, he retains his position unless found guilty beyond a reasonable doubt. In that case, the family may move to a different church if they believe their child, or they may leave because they don't believe their child and they are embarrassed by her accusations. In another scenario, the priest or pastor puts both overt and covert pressure on the child to recant and the family to leave. Smear campaigns are common.

What happens when a child discloses abuse by a family member? The mother faces one of the most difficult decisions of all. Does she believe her child and call the police on a husband, father, grandfather, uncle, or brother? Unfortunately, the most common scenario is that the mother goes into denial. Then, the child again faces intense pressure to recant, apologize for lying, and remain silent.

If the child is in a Christian family, she will likely be pressured to forgive the perpetrator. However, it is not possible for a young child to comprehend the extent of what has been done to her. Indeed, young children may practice learning to forgive with their peers, such as when a friend steals a toy. The adults have misplaced their priorities. The child must be protected and kept safe. Forgiveness may come later when the child is an adult and capable of making that type of decision. Forgiveness is for the healing of the survivor, not as a means for the abuser to get back his position in the Church or the family.

The critical issue is the veracity of the child. Still, it is extremely rare for a young child to lie about child sexual abuse. Once the accusation is made, a lot of effort will be put into investigating and exonerating the alleged perpetrator. Very little effort is typically put into a child-centric approach that respects her decision to speak up, respects her experience, and respects her need for safety.

Civil society has put into place many mechanisms that spring into play when a child discloses sexual abuse. These are legal, educational, institutional, medical and public policy mechanisms. Medical and forensic protocols are established. Teachers and school administrators are trained to identify the psychosocial signs of child sexual abuse. Governments have official policies and prescribed actions that must be applied. Hotlines exist. And the public discourse has become much more open in recent decades. The media, government agencies, academia, and other groups participate in conferences and discussions on what to do about childhood sexual abuse.

Even with these safety nets in place and a growing public awareness of the problem, the knee-jerk response when hearing a child's allegations is denial. Those closest to the child immediately believe the child must be lying.

Yet, Jesus tells us, "See that you do not despise one of these little ones. For I tell you that their angels in heaven always see the face of my Father in heaven." Matthew 18:10

Therefore, the first response must be to believe the child. The boy or girl must be treated with consideration for the great physical and psychic harm that has happened. The adults must stay open minded and listen carefully.

Why Do Children Lie?

In most cases, children lie to hide something. Fear is the motivation. They fear someone or something. They fear if they tell the truth, they will be punished, mocked, and/or not believed. This is what happens with childhood sexual abuse. A child hides the abuse because they fear being punished or not believed. They may have been threatened by the perpetrator.

The child who does report CSA will retract their disclosure when faced with disbelief and pressure from adults to do so. This produces enormous anxiety and fear in the child. The child fears more than the molester. She fears the adults who have the responsibility to protect her. She fears abandonment, which may affect her entire life.

What Children Do Not Lie About

Children will lie about things they should have done but didn't (homework), if they have legitimately wronged another person, such as bullying, or done something they should not have done like stealing.

These circumstances have a social desirability factor. Children lie in these situations because the know that the behaviors are not acceptable and they fear punishment if they told the truth. Children lie about sexual abuse for the same reasons. They sense that sexual behaviors are not socially acceptable. Thus, it is far more likely that a child will lie about being abused even when it is the truth, even when evidence points to the contrary. This means that when a child does disclose sexual abuse, they are more likely than not to be telling the truth.

Do Children Make Up Fairy Tales About Sexual Abuse?

Children under the age of 12 are not emotionally, cognitively, or physiologically prepared for sexual behaviors. They have little awareness about sex and sexuality. It makes no sense to suggest that a young child can make up a story about something he knows little to nothing about. When a young child exhibits behaviors that look sexual, it is a red flag to further investigate. Perhaps they witnessed some sexual activity or someone performed sexual activities on them. Rather than blaming the child, the adults must carefully follow up.

In addition, because young children do not typically know about sex and sexuality, they know that they suffered physical pain and injury, but they do not typically associate the abuse with sexuality. There is no awareness of the exploitation especially if the perpetrator made the effort to groom them. Older children have an awareness of the cultural aspects of sex that can be shame oriented, such as touching private parts. This feeling is stronger in adolescents making them even less willing to disclose. If they do disclose, they are likely telling the truth despite strong feelings of fear and shame.

In short, there is far more to demotivate a child to report sexual abuse than there is to motivate him or her to disclose. The pressure for silence is intense. The initial response to disbelieve the child does irreparable harm.

This is where the Church must hold to scripture. The Church must not despise the child. And, the Church must be the exemplary standard for the civil mechanisms designed to protect victims of child sexual abuse. The first thing a pastor or priest should do is notify the police so a proper investigation can begin.

Jesus said many things about children.

"If anyone causes one of these little ones—those who believe in me—to stumble, it would be better for them to have a large millstone hung around their neck and to be drowned in the depths of the sea. Matthew 18:6

"Let the little children come to me, and do not hinder them, for the kingdom of God belongs to such as these. Luke 18:16

"In the same way your Father in heaven is not willing that any of these little ones (children) should perish." Matthew 18:14

Our society has responded to child sexual abuse in many appropriate ways in the medical, legal, and psychosocial systems we rely upon. However, the greatest gap is that child sexual abuse happens primarily in the home and immediate social surroundings. Sexual abuse occurs in secret, in hiding, without witnesses. Many of our secular institutions fail to pick up on the warning signs. They hesitate to follow up because they are worry about lawsuits. Again, this is precisely where the Church must be the leader. All Christians are in the same family, and we must do as Jesus commanded.

The first step in doing that is to believe the young child who speaks up. He or she must then be protected from being alone with the alleged perpetrator. In many cases, the child might need to be separated completed from the alleged perpetrator. Such separation and protection are best done by the police and justice system. If the abuser is the father, then the mother may need to have him removed from the home (restraining order), or she may need to leave and seek shelter and help. Ideally, the Church should be her haven, but we know from experience that this is not currently occurring. Law enforcement will conduct its investigations without preconceptions or bias. Regardless of the outcome, the initial response must be to protect the child, and that comes from believing the disclosure.

We recognize that in this modern world many child molesters have ways to manipulate children and strike fear into them to ensure their silence. They also have alcohol and drugs at their disposal to knock a child unconscious so that there is no memory.

In these cases, we suspect that an occasional misidentification may happen. Still, the appropriate response is to believe the child and investigate. The response of the alleged perpetrator will be very telling. When hearing that they must separate from the child, the response should not be one of indignation and anger. Scripture tells us how a true parent acknowledges real harm to his son or daughter. The account is so famous, the phrase "split the baby" is part of our common lexicon.

For those not familiar with the story, it is during King Solomon's reign over Israel sometime between approximately 1000 to 962 B.C.E.

"Now two prostitutes came to the king and stood before him. One of them said, "Pardon me, my lord. This woman and I live in the same house, and I had a baby while she was there with me. The third day after my child was born, this woman also had a baby. We were alone; there was no one in the house but the two of us.

"During the night this woman's son died because she lay on him. So, she got up in the middle of the night and took my son from my side while I your servant was asleep. She put him by her breast and put her dead son by my breast. The next morning, I got up to nurse my son—and he was dead! But when I looked at him closely in the morning light, I saw that it wasn't the son I had borne."

The other woman said, "No! The living one is my son; the dead one is yours."

But the first one insisted, "No! The dead one is yours; the living one is mine." And so they argued before the king.

The king said, "This one says, 'My son is alive and your son is dead,' while that one says, 'No! Your son is dead and mine is alive.'"

Then the king said, "Bring me a sword." So, they brought a sword for the king. He then gave an order: "Cut the living child in two and give half to one and half to the other."

The woman whose son was alive was deeply moved out of love for her son and said to the king, "Please, my lord, give her the living baby! Don't kill him!"

But the other said, "Neither I nor you shall have him. Cut him in two!"

Then the king gave his ruling: "Give the living baby to the first woman. Do not kill him; she is his mother."

When all Israel heard the verdict the king had given, they held the king in awe, because they saw that he had wisdom from God to administer justice." Kings 3:16-28

The real mother put her baby's safety first even if it meant losing her child. Those who want to follow scripture's guidance must do the same. And this guidance is at least three thousand years old.

If a man has been falsely accused or accused in a case of misidentification, the appropriate course of action is to remove himself from the presence of the child and hire a competent attorney. Any man who is in this situation has every right and need to a defense. We don't argue against that at all. But, if he wants what is right for the child, then he will forgo contact until all has been resolved, which may take years in our system of jurisprudence. The godly parent will put his child's well-being first.

Mothers Who Deny

Most child sexual abuse is committed by close male family members: fathers, stepfathers, uncles, grandfathers, older brothers. Our society has progressed significantly over the last several decades to acknowledge a problem that is increasingly going public. However, the biggest obstacle standing in the way of justice is frequently a mother in denial. Some have called for mothers who fail to intervene and stop sexual abuse of their children to be found complicit and face criminal charges.

Denial incapacitates a mother when she is confronted with the possibility that her husband, bother, or father molested her child. In fact, the psychological state of denial can be so strong that the mother will not even consciously know that sexual abuse is occurring despite red flags. Even when confronted with clear evidence that sexual abuse is taking place, denial prevents her from intervening. Thus, the abuse may continue for years.

What is this psychological phenomenon of denial? Let's take a look at some basics of the issue. Denial is a psychological defense mechanism that filters out realities and painful feelings that overwhelm us. When a mother goes into denial despite evidence that a child is being sexually abused, she separates herself from responsibility, feelings of anger and betrayal towards the perpetrator, and her intense feelings of guilt at having failed to provide protection for her offspring.

A mother's denial may be intensified by her dependence on the molester if that man is her partner. As Roland Summit, who proposed Child Sexual Abuse Accommodation Syndrome in 1983, said,

> "as someone substantially dependent on the approval and generosity of the father, the mother in the incestuous triangle is confronted with a mind-splitting dilemma. ... Either the child ... or the father is ...lying and unworthy of trust. The mother's whole security and life adjustment and much of her sense of adult self-worth demand a trust in the reliability of her partner. To accept the alternative means annihilation of the family and a large piece of her own identity."

In plain English, the mother feels immense shock to discover she married a child molester. She is now confronted with a horrible decision. Believe the man, or believe her child. Whether or not she can provide financially for her family without the man compounds the dilemma. In addition, if she leaves and takes the children to protect them, she may face significant ostracism from the man's family and her own family, who may feel a divorce disgraces the family. The reality that her child is being sexually molested may bring up memories of being a victim of incest herself. The pain is too great.

Some mothers maintain denial even when confronted with incontrovertible evidence. The molester typically displays inappropriate behaviors before the actual incest begins like efforts to see the child naked, sleeping with the child in the same bed, exhibition of his own naked body, or excessive physical contact.

In some cases, a teenage child may produce photos or video, which can be so ubiquitous in our modern, connected-device world. While the mother may initially acknowledge the abuse, she may quickly sink into denial again, even blaming and smearing the victim. In a very real sense, the mother sacrifices her child in order to maintain financial support and a semblance of respectability. If the child makes the accusations to a mandatory reporter and her mother continues to place her child in harm's way, that child will likely end up in the foster care system.

Scripture is clear on the issue of sacrificing our children. In ancient Israel's neighbor, Canaan, physical child sacrifice was an appalling practice. We believe that child sexual abuse is a form of physical sacrifice of a child when it is allowed to happen even after it becomes known. It is a form of psychic and spiritual sacrifice.

The books of Deuteronomy and Jeremiah address child sacrifice this way:

> "The Lord your God will cut off before you the nations you are about to invade and dispossess. But when you have driven them out and settled in their land, and after they have been destroyed before you,

be careful not to be ensnared by inquiring about their gods, saying, "How do these nations serve their gods? We will do the same." You must not worship the Lord your God in their way, because in worshiping their gods, they do all kinds of detestable things the Lord hates. They even burn their sons and daughters in the fire as sacrifices to their gods." Deuteronomy 12:29-31

"The people of Judah have done evil in my eyes, declares the Lord. They have set up their detestable idols in the house that bears my Name and have defiled it. They have built the high places of Topheth in the Valley of Ben Hinnom to burn their sons and daughters in the fire—" Jeremiah 7:30-31

We must put the children first. We must act quickly, and we must follow scripture precisely to help end the pain.

The weight of pain, sorrow, and torment are palpable when you listen to a victim of child sexual abuse. It is especially difficult when that victim agonizes about forgiving the abuser to follow Christ's commandments.

Common questions arise. Doesn't Jesus teach us to forgive? What is the right thing to do?

Many psychologists, social workers, and others who work with victims of abuse know that it takes tremendous courage to leave an abusive relationship. But, in cases of child sexual abuse, the child has no means to leave. The child must depend on the other adults around him or her to force a separation, to force the abuser away.

In addition, those adults must understand that a child most likely does not fully understand the harm that has been done and have an immature view of what it means to forgive. They hear about forgiveness and know that Christians value this act.

Forgiveness by God's people toward one another is a central message. Where we go wrong is in defining who God's people are. A pedophile priest or pastor or any church member who commits child sexual abuse does not belong in the congregation. Scripture is clear on that issue.

Forgiveness is healing to the soul of the forgiver. For a child, that forgiveness may only come about after years of maturation and understanding. In the meantime, the adults in the church must protect the children against the abusers. Justice must be done. Without it, forgiveness in these situations may never come.

In Luke 17, Jesus speaks of forgiveness, but he also points to the consequences of abuse. He says that causing harm to another has deep consequences for the offender. We must always remember that in cases of sexual abuse and violence, restoration of the relationship typically is a great risk of danger for the victim. Forgiveness offers freedom, but reconciliation risks continued abuse. Forgiveness does not require that a survivor have any contact with the abuser.

Forgiveness is not a momentary whim. It is not a path of denial. Forgiveness is the narrow road to freedom. Forgiveness does not come from the victim because of a perpetrator's demands. It does not come from a victim because of dogmatic demands of the church. Forgiveness is hard won only after justice has been done. Then, and only then, can healing begin.

About the Authors

Deanna Christian is a neighborhood Chaplain living in Bowling Green, Kentucky, where she is a member of the Cumberland Presbyterian Church. She earned her Master's Degree in Biblical Studies from Fuller Theological Seminary and a teaching certificate from Western Washington University. She has worked in inner-city missions with the Presbytery of Seattle and rescued people sold into slavery in Southeast Asia who ended up in brothels or on the streets of America. She has taught English as a Second Language and is the Director of the Blessings Doll Project, a Kentucky non-profit that gives dolls to cancer patients. She currently ministers to survivors of the December 10th, 2021 Kentucky tornado and to Afghan women who escaped when Kabul fell. You can contact Deanna directly by calling 270-938-4679.

Wendy Hoke is the author of *The Bishop's Cross*. She was the victim of child sexual abuse by her grandfather, Konrad Koosmann, who was a Bishop in the American Lutheran Church.

She has been a content curator, social media manager, and blogger for over 10 years. She provides her writing services independently, and you can contact her through her website, wendyhoke.com.

She began her writing career while working at a top 10 Wall Street investment banking firm, where she researched and penned a weekly, compliance-approved newsletter detailing the events of the tax-exempt securities market. Subsequently, she moved from Wall

Street to Main Street as a senior manager for The Navy Exchange, a $2 billion retailer with operations across the globe including the U.S., Europe, Asia, and Iceland. After leaving her position as a civilian employee of the U.S. Navy, she briefly worked for the Marine Corps Exchange.

In addition, Wendy has been involved in her community by volunteering with Rady Children's Hospital Auxiliary raising money for social services for pediatric oncology patients. For 18 years, she participated in the Ocean Beach Community Dinners mission, which has fed the homeless for over 35 years.

She enjoys hiking, camping, golf, tennis, and cooking. Her faith is an integral part of her life, and she is an active member of a local Christian church.

Acknowledgments

The authors wish to thank and acknowledge the contribution made by Melanie Jula Sakoda. She wrote the section on sexual abuse within the Orthodox church. Deanna and Wendy appreciate the history and level of detail that she provided.

In 1999, Melanie Sakoda and two friends began a website to reach out to survivors of abuse in the Orthodox Christian churches. The three women all had close relatives who were abused in Orthodox settings. SNAP was always a valuable resource in their work and in 2008, Melanie and one of the women affiliated with the larger group. Melanie currently works for SNAP as its Survivor Support Coordinator.

www.ingramcontent.com/pod-product-compliance
Lightning Source LLC
LaVergne TN
LVHW052001060526
838201LV00059B/3778